I sleep 4-5 hours a night and that's plenty, because the nights I don't sleep there is a higher calling telling me to stand guard.

Torpedoes of truth.

I don't think people are prepared for the messages I'm delivering with violent love.

Once I exercise, I get my tiger-blood boiling. And then it's on.

Let's just say that, cosmically, things arranged themselves to direct me to this entity that is Philadelphia.

I have a disease?
Bullshit. I cured it
with my brain.

You can't process me
with a normal brain.

Pain is a myth.

I'm an F-18, bro. I will destroy you in the air and I will deploy my ordinance to the ground.

I'm not bi-polar. I'm bi-winning.

I am on a drug, it's called Charlie Sheen. It's not available because if you try it you will die. Your face will melt off and your children will weep over your exploded body.

I will win the war with
CBS with zeal, focus
and violent hatred.

I love Mel Gibson
He's great and a
beautiful man.

[Speaking about porn star Kacey Jordan] She's a retarded zombie.

I'm topical for the
next billion years.

Choose your Vice.

The last time I used?
What do you mean?
I used my toaster this
morning.

I closed my eyes and made it so with the power of my mind, and unlearned 22 years of fiction...the fiction of AA.

Well, I mean, first of
all come Wednesday
morning they're
going to rename it
Charlie Bros. and not
Warner Bros.

[On John Stamos possibly replacing him on Two and a Half Men] I like John, but he doesn't have what I have and the show sucks if he's on it.

I have a 10,000 year-old brain and the boogers of a 7 year-old. That's how I describe myself.

Can't is the cancer of happening.

There's been a tsunami of media, and I've been riding it on a mercury surfboard.

I'm different. I have a different constitution, I have a different brain, I have a different heart. I got tiger blood, man.

[About P Diddy] Get dressed my man, I'm sending the driver!

I will not follow a certain path because it was written for normal people. People who aren't special. People who don't have tiger blood and Adonis DNA.

If you're a part of my family, I will love you violently.

There's a new
sheriff in town
and he has an
army of assassins.

I'm not Thomas Jefferson.
He was a pussy.

[On the two Goddesses]
We form, what you'd call, a wedge.

I mean, what's not to love? Especially when you see how I party man, it's epic.

I was bangin' seven-
gram rocks and finish-
ing them because that's
how I roll. I have one
speed, one gear.

You've read about the goddesses, come on. They're an international sensation.

I tried marriage. I'm 0 for 3 with the marriage thing. So, being a ballplayer, I believe in numbers. I'm not going 0 for 4. I'm not wearing a golden sombrero.

All my guys friends are gonna throw tomatoes at me. It's like an organic union of the hearts.

These are my girl friends.
These are the women that
I love that have completed
the three parts of my
heart. It's a polygamy story.

All we do is put wins
in the record books.
We win so radically
in our underwear
before our first cup
of coffee, it's scary.

[Talking about Life]
It's perfect. It's awesome. Every day is just filled with just wins.

I have spent, I think, close to the last decade effortlessly and magically converting your tin cans into pure gold.

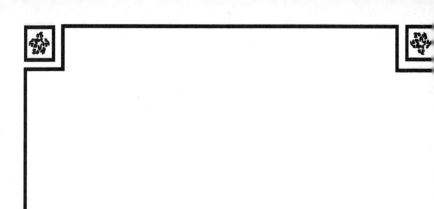

Dying's for fools.

People say it's lonely
at the top, but I sure
like the view.

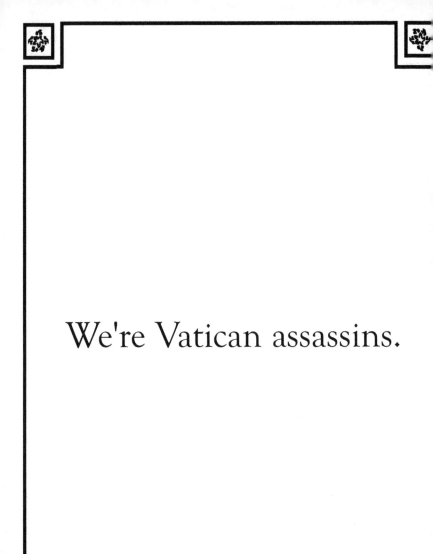

We're Vatican assassins.

We work for the pope,
we murder people.

I guess I'm just that God damn bitchin'.

[Guns] I don't own any anymore. They took them all away...That's another story.

I'm tired of pretending
I'm not a total bitchin'
rock star from Mars.

I can't make up a hernia.
That's just lame.

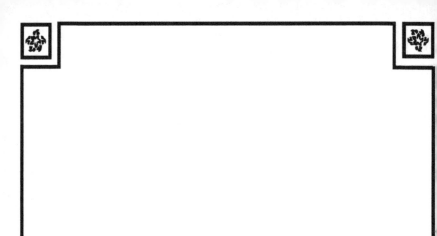

CBS picked a fight
with a warlock.

I don't understand
what I did wrong
except live a life that
everyone is jealous of.

The wildfires are spreading. The meek are scattering.

One of my favorite
poets is Eminem.

I've got tiger blood, man.

Duh, winning! It's like, guys, IMDB right there, 62 movies and a ton of success. I mean come on, bro.

The title of my book has finally been delivered through vast and extensive Lunar channels. 'Apocalypse Me' or Warlock Latin for WINNING.

Just got invited to do the Nancy Grace Show. I'd rather go on a long road trip with Chuck Lorre in a '75 Pacer.

CBS Owes me an apology. A big one. While licking my feet.

There are parts of me
that are Dennis Hopper.

Look what I'm dealing with, man. I'm dealing with fools and trolls.

[About Bree Olson, porno star and Penthouse Pet]
I chipped one of my warlock fangs on a great white shark I had to murder. Pissed me off and like an ass I tool kit out on her.

I'm celebrating me,
every day.

I live inside the truth,
and you cannot
debate me.

Sorry my life is so much more bitchin' than yours. I planned it that way.

I don't know, winning,
anyone? Rhymes with
winning? Anyone?
Yeah, that would be us.

Panic is for amateurs and morons.

You already own you.
Now go earn the
power. Earn the
Truth. Earn the most
important compo-
nent in this entire
dimension, yourself.

I have absolute rocket-fuel in my veins. That's why people just can't figure me out.

[On CBS and Chuck Lorre] They're soft Targets in cheap suits. Amateurs.

I think I'm worth
over a 100 billion
dollars, but that's just
on a cellular level.

You have the right to kill me, but you do not have the right to judge me. Boom! That's the whole movie. That's life.

Come on, bro. I won "best picture" at 20. I wasn't even trying. I wasn't even warm.

The only thing I'm addicted to right now is winning.

[On Chuck Lorre. Writer and producer on Two and a Half Men] Clearly I have defeated this earth-worm with my words.

I'm not 'aw shucks'.
Because I'm gnarly.

[When questioned about porn stars] They're the best at what they do and I'm the best at what I do, and together...it's on.

The run I was on made Sinatra, Flynn, Jagger, Richards. All of them just look like droopy-eyed, armless children.

CHAPTER 2

CHARLIE, HERE'S SOME IDEAS FOR FUTURE QUOTES

You can dissect me, puree me, or spin dry me, but you still won't comprehend what I'm saying, because you're a Swiffer dry mop weeping alone in the utility closet waiting for mommy to put dust particles on you.

You'll be sucking down my jet stream while your grandmother's limbs fall off, explode and demolish all the children of the world including frail pasty white boys that live in their auntie's laundry basket.

Don't you get it people?!
I eat Twinkies and crap
out galaxies where all
the apartments comes
furnished. You just have
to fluff dry your
own socks.

Tonight, get into your jammies, pull the covers over your head and peer into that soft wad you call your brain and you know what you will see?....Me, staring at the back of your eyeballs, staring at me, staring at the back of your eyeballs and on and on forever.

My head's already in atomic sub particle mode, and you only exist in my cerebral cortex because there were no vacancies in that scrumptious blob of beef jerky doctors call my liver.

My right testicle has more testosterone flowing through it than all the organisms on the planet combined, from a tiny paramecium to a big sweet gnarly Kodiak Bear.

God was invented so I could point a finger at him and say stop cutting in line bro.

When Mother
Hubbard goes to your
cupboard, she finds
squat. In my
cupboard there is me,
Moses squared.

I'm dressed in a bullet proof moo moo. And yes if I pull it over my head you can see that I have a mini-bar strapped to my chest.

People want to know
what makes me tick,
well I would invite
you inside and give
you the grand tour,
but you will probably
chock to death while
you're frantically
guzzling down my
essence.

If I was a Greek God, the citizens of Athens would be motor crossing up my butt just so they could be incinerated by the billion exploding suns which reside in my colon.

Go ahead touch me. If you're lucky maybe you'll catch my disease and that disease will melt your eyes, and drench the garden gnomes of the world in pure candy goodness.

I'm starting to replicate, so stand back children cause daddy has a brand new bag filled with nuclear submarines, drones and sticky buns.

I wasn't born, I was
extrapolated from the
mind of headless
Iraqi boy who had to
crawl over the
corpses of his dead
parents just to drink
the Cool Aid.

Don't piss me off, because while your mother is changing your diapers I will vaporize all the troglodytes that are doing wheelies on your subprime mortgages.

When I say fugliness is killing more American's than cancer, car accidents and Malaria combined, I say it with the force of a zillion pre-teen girls slapping each other in the face with oven mitts.

If you took every Jimi Hendrix riff he ever played or dreamed of and put them in a thimble it wouldn't be one-millionth as melodic as the sound of one of my farts.

You know what CBS stands for?.... Cosmic Boy Syndrome or Cold Bloody Socks, your choice.

Made in the USA
Middletown, DE
16 February 2023